O9-AIC-226

BELMONT PUBLIC LIBRARY

is for BROOKLYN

SELINA ALKO

Christy Ottaviano Books
Henry Holt and Company • New York

MAP OF BROOKLYN

Williamsburg Bridge

East River

Brooklyn Bridge

Manhattan Bridge

Hudson River

Greenpoint

Williamsburg

Bushwick

DUMBO

Brooklyn Heights

Brooklyn Navy Yard

Cobble Hill

DOWNTOWN BROOKLYN

Clinton Hill

Fort Greene

Bedford-Stuyvesant

Cypress Hills

Red Hook

Carroll Gardens

Boerum Hill

GOWANUS

PROSPECT HEIGHTS

Crown Heights

BROWNSVILLE

East New York

Park Slope

PROSPECT PARK

GREEN-WOOD CEMETERY

WINDSOR TERRACE

East Flatbush

Sunset Park

Canarsie

BAY RIDGE

KENSINGTON

Flatbush

Flatlands

DYKER HEIGHTS

Borough Park

Midwood

MARINE PARK

MILL BASIN

BERGEN BEACH

Fort Hamilton

Bensonhurst

GERRITSEN BEACH

Verrazano-Narrows Bridge

BATH BEACH

Sheepshead Bay

SEA GATE

CONEY ISLAND

BRIGHTON BEACH

Gravesend

MANHATTAN BEACH

Atlantic Ocean

Author's Note

BROOKLYN is awash in history. It is the most populous borough in New York City, home to millions of immigrants. There's so much unique to Brooklyn that it was impossible to fit its complete heritage and landscape into one book. Some things scream BROOKLYN but no longer exist, such as Ebbets Field and the Brooklyn Dodgers baseball team, and yet they remain an essential part of the borough's collective history. Many Brooklyn icons and institutions are vibrantly part of the cultural landscape, such as the famous eateries Nathan's and Junior's and, of course, the Cyclone roller coaster at Coney Island. Each page in this book is a collage of elements, much like the eclectic nature of Brooklyn itself. The depictions are not necessarily realistic. For example, don't expect to ride the F train to Fort Greene just because they both appear on the same page! I hope this journey from A to Z puts you in a Brooklyn state of mind.

Crossing the bridge from Manhattan to Brooklyn fills me with excitement but, at the same time, also relaxes me. When my husband, illustrator Sean Qualls, lured me to Brooklyn some ten years ago, I was instantly seduced. It has been a thrill to discover so many amazing neighborhoods, landmarks, cultural happenings, and hip cafés. It's also nice to have more physical "home" space. The horizontal landscape affords things like small yards, neighborhood barbecues, and frequent visits to community playgrounds. Plus there are trees—lots of them! It's the ideal environment for me to stay inspired. Whether I'm with my family sitting on our stoop or strolling along the boardwalk, I feel perfectly at home in world-renowned Brooklyn.

BROOKLYN BRIDGE

BROWNSTONES

BAM
BROOKLYN ACADEMY OF MUSIC

BOTANIC GARDEN

BASEBALL

Brooklyn College

BRIGHTON BEACH

BORSCHT

BOARDWALK

EASTERN PARKWAY

E
EGG CREAMS

EBBETS FIELD

ELEVATED TRAINS

FOURTH AVE

100

F

EY AND

F TRAIN

F TRAIN

Best Sellers The New York Times

FICTION

by Jim Butcher

series about

FULTON FERRY LANDING

GREENPOINT

BAKERY

G train

GREEN·WOOD CEMETERY

graffiti

G

GOWANUS CANAL

GRAND ARMY PLAZA

Immigrants

ICE CREAM TRUCKS

ice cream

ITALIAN ICE

Intellectuals

ICE-SKATING

JITNEY-STYLE CABS

CELEBRATE
BROOKLYN!

LONG ISLAND RAIL ROAD

Lox
+
BAGELS
L

BROOKLYN PUBLIC LIBRARY

LIBRARY

Lemon
Ice

LEFFERTS GARDENS

Nathan's SINCE 1916 ® 99

NAVY YARD

N NEIGHBORHOODS

Newsstands

New York U S A

N TRAIN

BQE

{BROOKLYN-QUEENS EXPRESSWAY}

Q TRAIN

Q Q TRAIN

R

RED HOOK

BANYA

RUSSIAN BATHS

GOOD FORK

HOPE & ANCHOR

Restaurants

ROW HOUSES

POST

400

Recycling

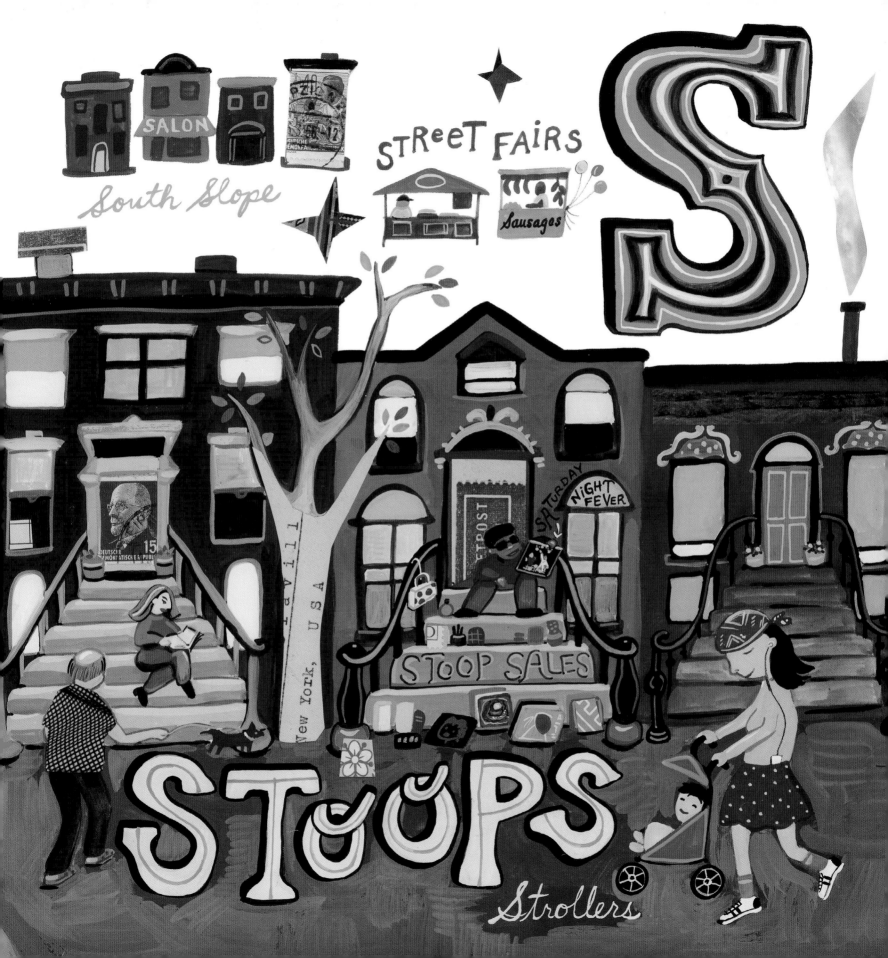

TREES

A Tree Grows in BROOKLYN

TURNSTILES

TROLLEYS

T

tokens

T TRANSIT MUSEUM

AVENUE U

USS BROOKLYN

unicycles

1964

SUBWAY SUBWAY

www.mta.info/museum

5655

YIELD TO

Museum

5

CHE REPUBLIK

SUBWAY: 2 3 4 5*

5655

UNDERGROUND U

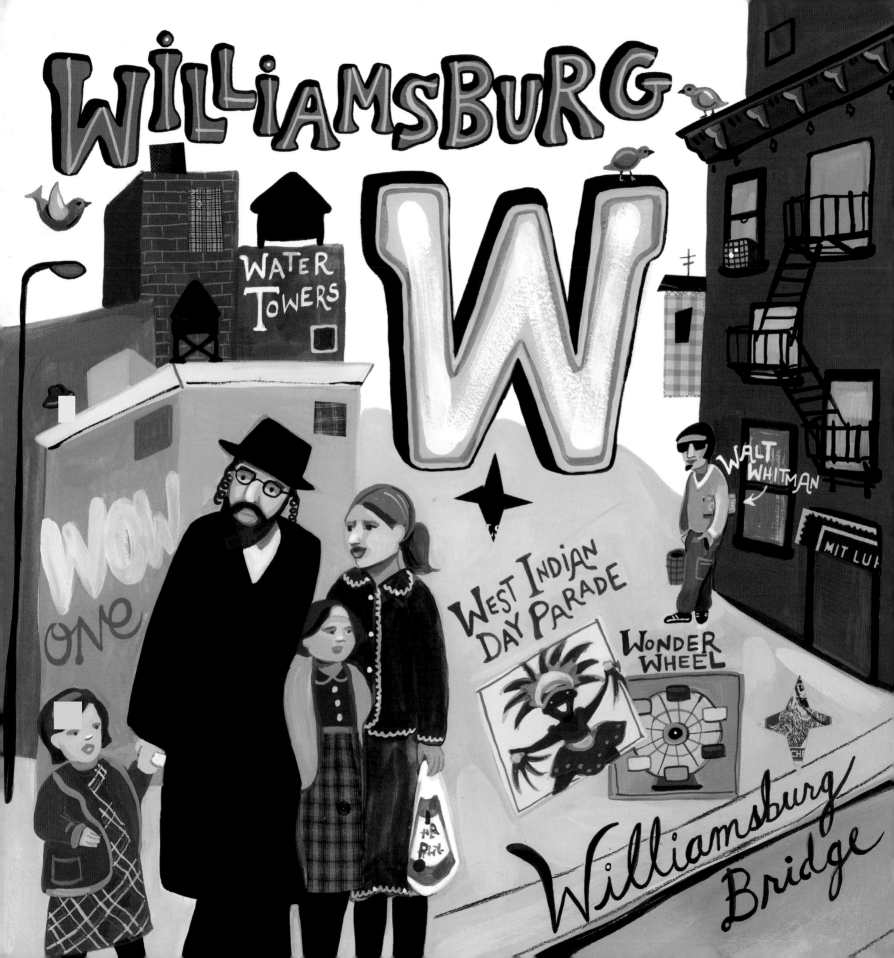

Z

zoo

zzzzzzZZ

PROSPECT PARK ZOO

J
PIC
ALK

To my Brooklyn friends and families:
This book is for each and every one of you!

With special thanks to former Brooklynite
Christy O, editor extraordinaire

Henry Holt and Company, LLC
Publishers since 1866
175 Fifth Avenue
New York, New York 10010
mackids.com

Henry Holt® is a registered trademark of Henry Holt and Company, LLC.
Copyright © 2012 by Selina Alko
All rights reserved.

Library of Congress Cataloging-in-Publication Data
Alko, Selina.
B is for Brooklyn / by Selina Alko. — 1st ed.
p.   cm.
"Christy Ottaviano Books."
ISBN 978-0-8050-9213-4 (hc)
1. Brooklyn (New York, N.Y.)—Juvenile literature. 2. New York (N.Y.)—Juvenile literature.
3. Alphabet books. I. Title.
F129.B7.A45 2012   974.7'23—dc23   2011028595

First Edition—2012
Gouache and collage on Arches watercolor paper
were used to create the illustrations for this book.
Printed in China by South China Printing Co. Ltd.,
Dongguan City, Guangdong Province

1 3 5 7 9 10 8 6 4 2